Like That
New and Selected Poems

Like That

New and Selected Poems

Sybil Pittman Estess

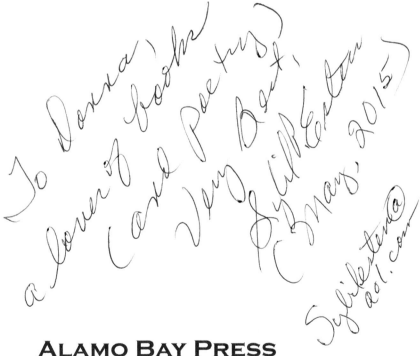

To Donna,
a lover of books
(and Poetry)
Very Best,
Sybil Pittman Estess
Xmas, 2015
Sylvestex@
aol.com

ALAMO BAY PRESS

SEADRIFT · AUSTIN

Front Cover Photo: Wallpapers
Back Cover Artwork: Julian Brashears
Author Photo: Ted Estess
Book Design: ABP

For orders and information:
Alamo Bay Press
Pamela Booton, Director
825 W 11th Ste 114
Austin, Texas 78701
pam@alamobaypress.com
www.alamobaypress.com
www.alamobaywritersworkshop.com

Library of Congress Control Number: 2014957994
ISBN: 978-0-9908632-2-9

For

Himma Lynn Estess

and

Zollie Be Estess

Contents

from *Manuevers*

from *Labyrinth*

from *Blue, Candled in January Sun*

from *Seeing the Desert Green*

Epilogue

New Poems

Parting

(Roy Simmons Estess: January 5, 1939-June 25, 2010)

In their small south-Mississippi hometown,
my husband hugs his brother. Pats his face
in the casket. "Don't leave me now. Please
don't!" he weeps. Bees killed Troy. He was
mowing on a tractor, on a Friday, in late June.
Troy died in ten minutes. Before the hot funeral,
three days later, we went to see the unparalleled
personality's body. No wake, no family gathers
in any of several private, available funeral rooms.
Troy's body is stored in an office, "to keep it cooler."
One woman clerk keeps coming in, pulling out
drawers, banging and fumbling to get paperclips or staples.
The man running the place, Jimmy Boyd, in his
drawl says, "It's time t'git on go. We gotta load
him up fer the church." Once there, hundreds
wait to see. No chance for the only two siblings
to be alone. It's nearly a state funeral in a country
town. Seven eulogies. First my husband's, then
the Director of NASA's, the astronauts' (never seen
before in person in this hamlet) and on and on. One
had been on Apollo 13. It all lasts three hours.
After the procession from the burial, there's fried
chicken, ham, southern peas, cornbread, homemade
cakes at the church hall. All I could think about
was that before, back at the house, I had asked
my spouse if he wanted to go to Troy alone, to be
by himself with the only man who called him "Bro."
No. He wanted me to be with him, he said softly.
Once there, what I saw when in heat we reached
the cold office that held the body in a box was
bloodless, pale, stopped. Troy in life always moved
fast. His blood ran swift and parched. His hair was
parted for us and everyone at the sweltering church
to notice not the way he wore it, but on the wrong side.

Up

"Up" is one of the few words
my tiny nineteen-month-old
granddaughter knows, along
with "MaMa," "DaDa," "Agua,"

and "Bye Bye." She's only
high enough to come up to
our knees and has to look "up"
constantly. So she wants to

be "up" when she yearns to
be held, or cuddled, or read to.
To play. Rock. Sleep. "Up,"
she says when she has enough

of her breakfast or lunch, or then
supper. "Up," she repeats as she
walks up the stairs, holding onto
her grandfather or me, and also

the railing. Even when she goes down,
she says, "Up." It's "Up"
when she climbs like a mite-
spider onto the adult sofa or

chairs. It seems that "down"
would come soon, since she
knows "DaDa" with its "Ds."
But what she desires now is

"up." Then "Up" and "Up"—
Always her current way of moving.
It may be months, years, or a
lifetime before she has to learn

Sybil Pittman Estess

the meaning of going the opposite
direction, going "down": "Delve,"
"Depths," "Disappointment" or just
"Do." Do it now. Go downward,

Himma. Not all good is "up."

Edge

(Esalen, Big Sur, California: May, 2010)

California's broken, Seattle's Nasdaq
is unsafe. Portland's hills on the river
have ceased building. La Jolla's lures

have too many Chicanos along seashore
with its blooming red roses. Libraries
are closed. Yet one spot by the redwoods,

on water, is still sanctified, sacred: Esalen.
North of Hearst Castle, south of Carmel
and Monterey. Twenty-five acres

of hot sulfur springs from rocks. Gardens
raised organically. Courses: "Neuro-
Scientific Way to Happiness." "The Neuro

Dharma of Love." "Tai Chi Easy." "Psycho
Pharmacology," "The Transformational
Enneagram," "Being Present to your life,"

"Romancing Spirit," "Spirit Medicine: Vision-
seeker II." "Don't Look for a Job, Create
a R.O.L.E." And if you ditch your clothes,

lie on these decks buck naked, butts or
breasts and bush up, after you have descended
the dusty hill to bathe, whether you are dirty,

divorced, unemployed, disabled, uneducated,
have just spent your life uptight, have or
have not smoked pot, you will be whole.

Sybil Pittman Estess

"Enchantment"

We float on a three-year-old sailboat,
"Enchantment," brought from Maine.

We leave from Long Island. By motor.
We moor in moonlight, an hour past

Port Jefferson. At midnight, waves
rock, cradle all of us. With open hatch,

we sleep in twin births. No cuddling.
Cold wind on water. The co-captain

couple inhabit main cabin. In night
I think: not many restore old crafts such

as this one, or pilot them now. Only
learned sailors comprehend "Geo-positioning

System." Or read satellites. Mark correct
coordinates on charts. But our two loving,

married mates do. She even with her MS
disease. They do not get lost, since they heed

all these angels. They use their depth-finders
diligently. They are aware: without careful

instruments, testing (how this relates to that),
anyone can run aground.... At daylight

with no dawn on Independence Day, for
six hours our boat points north, slowly.

We traverse the sound by same motor.
No sails, at six knots. Every craft today

creeps in fog, dangerously. We search
the precarious way over to shore for lost

land. *Meanwhile, my old love, all day I*
plumb our own depths, alone, by a means

few do. I read poems, collected, called
"On Love." Like this boat, these transport me

to new places. They are my sole means
to imagination, the one path through haze.

Mid-afternoon, with no warning, Connecticut
suddenly unveils—solid green marvel.

We are mysteriously there: July 4: a new country.
The third sea-day, we go north, toward Rhode

Island. I think how yesterday the fog, like
our lives, had been holding us back so long

from solid sun, bright, unbroken.
Mistiness finished, today Newport.

Sybil Pittman Estess

The Beach

A child plays on sand by waves
out my door at the motel in Galveston.

He pulls something—wagon? No, surfboard.
He waits for his brother to come. Then

he runs away fast, beyond my horizon.
It's 8:30, a Sunday morning.

I was one child in Florida more than
fifty years before. I was a girl, age nine

when Daddy first took us. He soon died. I am
always wayfaring to water. My place is

clear, aqua 1950s sand paradise. I still see
myself, waiting for my sister, and Daddy. I am

this child.

Returning: High Place on Lake

Nearly twenty summers here. Seven in our house
we built. We two imagined the "here" as if
heaven. As if we ourselves planed these pine

logs. You drew it, facing the water at nearly
9,000 feet. I collected carefully each furnishing
for two years in Houston, scavenged like a rat.

We built dams over any flood of disappointment,
like the beavers do who gnaw here. I envisioned
each of six rooms, what would go where: color,

texture, and theme. That January you ascended
to frozen paradise to prod builders. Two icy weeks
below zero you worked at their sides with hammer

and fur gloves. In May we moved in. I thought
I had never seen such glory, such an image become
life. It was everything we'd labored for. More. Today

I find nothing much external excites me. Not even
the entire Rocky Range, with its few ice peaks this July.
June's killing fires didn't touch me. (So what if it burns?)

Time with its happen stances has seared us too—like forest
crisps—with its refining blaze. Are outer views now
irrelevant? As your humorous dead brother once laughed,

"Body parts begin to fall off. They're not under
warranty." At seventy, like these huge Osprey
here, we dive deep to feed. We have mostly soul left.

Sybil Pittman Estess

On Leaving the Lake

We came in summer heat, through
drought and no campfires allowed.

We stayed through two weeks of Indian
fall with Aspen so gold and red they

could have been butter and fire. No rain,
so leaves lingered. My two bought trees

have not turned. I watered them daily.
Hummingbirds migrated to Mexico.

Yesterday, first snow on Rocky peaks.
Geese are paused on the lake. Crows

caw for the start of cold. Moose are now
sleuthing and elk are mostly across roads

in the National Park: hiding from hunters.
My red geraniums still bloom, and the purple

petunias we have to leave. No freezes
have come, although three fall frosts.

Fields are brown, ground cover is red.
Cafes and shops in town lock their doors.

Stores are beginning to sport skis, snow-
mobiles. Although I am still swimming daily

in the main lodge's heated pool, it closes
next week. Time to leave? Who can board

up this gorgeous plenty? We will drive south
now, to family, friends—what we call home.

How to Re-See

It was November 1
in Syracuse, New York, some
forty years ago.

Leaf colors had just passed.
Global warming had not
yet come. It was total

blue and clear sky. So I
wanted to take a walk.
Ground was so slightly

white. Air crisp enough I
could hear my own breath,
my crunch-steps on ground.

That day, all trees bare,
the big thermometer we sat
on the porch said zero, I recall.

Talons of the Holy Ghost

(In memory: Jane Blaffer Owen)

Thomas Merton claims that
When the Holy Spirit lifts us up, it's by

His claws. His talons. They dig
And they hurt. Do we want

It? Do we desire to rise above
Mire from which he might free us?

Or do we hope to stay stuck?
Are we eager for our skin

To rip, his tough beak break our
Hearts? Do you really yearn

To fly with Him, bleeding?

Mid-October

It's nearly dark but I am bathed
in sweat I'm so hot from buckets
of this work. Tomorrow no more
daylight savings time. This seems
the last hour of our wet, mosquito-
ridden heat. This citrus is not
from Key West, the Texas Valley,
Mexico, or the San Joaquin. No,
the Texas coast has just adjusted
to ice caps melting, polar bears
homeless, oceans rising, and
growing grapefruit, oranges,
lemons here now, easily. Few
freezes anymore. So today, I
picked prickly lemons, their
small thorns irritating my skin
and me. Neighborhood trees
are so laden they fall over on
their sides before January, when
due. My three trees, new and small,
are full of their fruit. Now is the time.

Across Waves

In thick, late blackness, she hopes he who was
with her once wonders what she may be saying

on another continent, so final and far away....
She imagines how his car is holding out, or

his elbow... his kids... what he has tasted
this year with his wife. In the likeness she holds,

his life is like a mirror. In her undying image,
she is kissing those toes, leg-backs, buttocks

in some familiar, chaste way. She's rubbing
his aching arm-bones. She knows only this:

he has grown older, fat, portly, maybe gray.
(Perhaps someday he will be at her funeral?)

He speaks another language tonight, even now.
No, she thinks, everything about them together

was all so very far-fetched—they both knew:
they were fastened.... But his lasting longing

she can't see. He uses his mind, mostly, to mend
desire. Before, by his body, he had nothing at all

except her smile—and what she seemed to see or say.
All that quick newness she was and offered freely.

Yesterday.

Song of Magdalene

Like that cast out Mary, she could remove
his shoes slowly. Then she would search
his sandals, soles, for clues to his heart.

She might notice all bones' malformations.
Each impediment on his toes would be there
to teach her of his dust and clay in old age.

She does not desire a lover who is young
or distant, unblemished—Adonis who would
woo her, take her off quickly to Shangri-La.

No, she wants a worn mortal, a mere man's
breath. Bruised, burned, his hands ripe,
his body lacking time. For him she wills

to loosen her hair. She will bathe
his feet and his soul forever
in warm, scented oil.

Houston: How We Pass Through

When Phil, my African-American
friend here who owned
the Texaco service station
at the corner of the bayou
and Calhoun St. a half mile
from our house, sold out (he had
"full service"—very rare here).
We both cried when we said
good-bye. We had had a past:
we had been confidantes about
my husband and his wife, fishing
in Mississippi, where I am from,
carburetors, all kinds of gaskets
and gasoline, strangers, even
his customers—one sexy white
woman kept coming in shorts,
sitting down, flirting with him.
(He always said, "Mama will
kill me.") But the sadness: we live
in mostly segregated sections. I am
white, am not welcome in his black.
I once went to his home. His wife
frowned. I was not invited to sit
down.... Now Mr. Gonzales, our
postman of thirty years secretly goes
into expected yet unacknowledged
retirement. Some folks in our small,
friendly neighborhood are making
him an appreciation basket, as if he had
died. He is dead to us. Where does he live?
We cannot guess. He is Hispanic. His house
is not near us. I know, since he told me he
has a food garden, with chickens, too. We
discuss it at my bright-blue door. And drought,

health, his hospitalization. Now he'll be
gone forever. Crossing these lines we still do not dare.

Magnolia Bayou: The House

So I am on my way back
from my errand and riding
through River Oaks, the posh
Houston super-rich not mansions
but palaces being built. They're
already there—quite amazing
yet not so beautiful as the pink
and purple and white and coral
azaleas in full March bloom.
Then I drive toward my own home, cross
Houston, cross the city via my route—
Alabama St—and round about Fannin
I hear on NPR that in Bay St. Louis,
Mississippi, this week a man (a Mr.
"LaRound" or some name like that,
who was interviewed) found an entirely
submerged house collapsed on itself
by Hurricane Katrina in Magnolia
Bayou. They pulled out an ice chest
and found an owner's name. She
is in Kentucky now, and her sons.
(Her man is nowhere to be found.)
So they gave her some of her silver
and china and crystal—not even broken,
and she is glad. And I am now in
the ghetto and everyone is black
on the streets and speaking of houses
I am near my own. I am disoriented
thinking of a house completely
submerged in Magnolia Bayou
in Bay St. Louis and can hardly find
my way home, especially since
the City of Houston has torn down
eight houses at my turning point
because of the metro coming five

blocks from our house, which some
think is very good, some very bad.
I do find the turn. I turn in. I locate
my house, not yet crumbled, red brick.
Not yet submerged. I do have a bayou
one block away. I do not have a River
Oaks castle or even a mansion. I have
a 1938 house, all very dry.

(Kids of various colors are playing
on the block in the March weather and
there is no wind. Just lush green now,
not hurricane season yet. Merely spring.)

Sybil Pittman Estess

The Happiness With Which it Ends

They liked each other a lot, but
she adored Santa Barbara and
San Diego. He grooved on Bangor,
Maine. While she sunbathed in
Key West, he longed to be riding
a bike in Stanley Park, Vancouver.
Or he chose New York, while she
drove around, happy, in L.A. Finally,
they decided to move to another
country. They tried Europe. She
was delighted by Greece and Sicily.
He loved Holland with The Hague
and also Scandinavia. He then
found Russia so enthralling but
she had a very hard time leaving
Egypt. Then they did Asia: he
adored Beijing. She could hardly
part from Bangalore. Their tastes
just seemed different, most
of the time. They knew they needed
to compromise. So they eventually
thought of living on the ocean. He
found the Atlantic his preference,
while she stubbornly always chose
the Pacific. They finally tried out
the Gulf of Mexico. And oh how
they were happy. No one could
ever say why. Their secret. Yet
they never ever had one argument
after they met there in the blue
waters and swam. Finally, "I am,"
she said. He said it too. They were.

Editing Life

Great gods! Who can do
it? Especially if one
has been a collector

of anything: books,
poems, china, rugs....
Who can throw away

what they once loved?
Who can discard photo-
graphs of persons gone?

What is one to do with
one's past, one's dear
treasures and trinkets?

Burn? Recycle? Pray
that you will not recall
them? Just pitch and

forget? Your life, your
loves, your life-lines
that fed you? What is

it to live in the moment
when you have had
so much, so many loves?

I Have a Pair of Earrings

from each vanished friend—Carla's silver,
Tanya's mother of pearl; Sue's butterfly
pin. Yet jewelry cannot bring flesh back, or

sound. Their voices. My friends are
somewhere burned to ashes, scattered
From Biscayne Bay to waterfalls in Georgia

to Texas dirt. To one I said, "Good luck" by phone,
never knowing she would bleed to death
tomorrow by her surgeon's knife. That shock

was not the same as just last Sunday's "Goodbye,
my dear one," the last that went, gray skin and
sunken eyes. Moaning lightly, squeezing my

fingers tightly with her bony and cold hands.
They took her away with quiet sirens the next noon.
Her neighbors came outside, so silent, all heads

bowed. Keep jewelry? When love is gone forever?
I wail three days for each. Fresh grief over,
I have earrings now. Just to remember them.

In Passing

How many before you have decorated
your house, or died here before you?

How many have loved this past or have
loathed their histories here? Who has

rested her body from a day's tedium?
Who has cooked here for cousins? For

farmers, perhaps, or MD's? Who made
her own bedspread here, taking five

years? Who quilted, neighbors always
helping her, in her front room? Who

took a photograph of whom? Assume
the house has outlasted weather, tornado,

wind and fire. The persons who labored
here passed first. But what will our kids

do with these buildings? Inherit? Inhabit?
Sell? Well, they could live on or re-invest

house-cash. They could lose it. Use it
or trash. This home you love, the place

you reared them, will pass on. The deed.
So all of your doings (including your books).

They may all pass to strangers. Even
your enemy could end up owning your

locks. Strange knobs and walls. Stranger
keys. Look at our snap-your-finger days

here. Think of them as your ways.

Hunt

He and I stalk through
brush in December. He
is looking for birds. I

notice the dried brush,
already frozen, exercise
we are getting, my step

father and I. He kills
a quail. I see how all
the leaves have fallen.

He listens and whistles.
He makes me look down
the barrel. Tells me how

to pull the trigger. I do
not want to do it. But
that night we have fried

and baked, and some
doves, the peace bird.
I can still hear them

cooing. No questioning
the male house authority.
We eat what he takes.

Squirrel

-1-

I always hated when Daddy had been
doing that. They were too fat, and
he cooked them with white rice.
But we did not question what father
said or served. He liked to cook.
There were no vegetables with "the mess."
And birds had little pocks where shot.
Broken blood vessels, meat bloody.
We would chew and swallow, silent.
(The bullets had all been picked out.)

-2-

My son said he killed many with
his BB and then air guns. All just
here and there around our Houston
house. We never saw them. Once,
he said he hit a bird—and he wrote
a poem about that death in high school.
He cried. Now he is doing the 12 Steps.
Number 4 in a moral inventory of his
thirty-three years. In writing. It's long.

Gun

We search and search,
my friend and I, trying
to find what I want to
kill—with all my memory.
We fail on Good Friday.
Finally, my husband says
where he put all except
the magazine: in a cabinet.

He saved my life. 4:00 a.m.,
front door. I'd never wanted
to do it. After my ringing
the bell, and his talking
and talking, he jumped me.
"Who sold you this god-
damned thing?" he yelled,
popping it open. (I'd never
known he knew anything
about guns.) "The pawn shop!"
I had one son, age eight....

When I finally find it, turn it
in to police at the local college,
I tell them a suicidal student
has left it in our home. "Oh,
we get these all the time,"
he says. "What do you do
with them?" I am curious.
"Grind them down, lady."

My life back, that was that.

Sybil Pittman Estess

Sonnet with Liberties: Violation

Long past, when you chose to take my hand—
a hard surprise—at the party we had both attended,
as the buffet courses ended, in the closed room,
at first I did not look in your face.

You squeezed my waist as your message:
"Everything mended." I thought then that
it was grace, erasing hurt. It was violation. Tiny care
lines creased your face. Your winter-white lace dress

matched your December-blonde hair. We two
chatted about your grown daughter, my young
son, your dead husband. Never my living one
in the living room. Unknowing guests snapped

us in snapshots. Cake came, with candles. Coffee.
Former best friend, you floated off, for just your cup.

Like That

"Christ will come like that," words spoken by the priest, upon seeing a peacock strut and show his colors. From "The Displaced Person" by Flannery O'Connor.

With finest foods and chocolates, a large family
sits around a long table on Easter at a Houston
upscale hotel. Love is here, including for new
male-female twins of two months. My own
granddaughter, two and a half years, half full
of M&Ms, from cracked plastic eggs. She scavenged
them at the church egg hunt and at this hotel. She
can sense cocoa and sugar any and everywhere.
That's what Easter is to her so far—cute new dress
and shoes.
      But for me, it was the service on Good
Friday night. Latin medieval music and slow readings
from a gospel about how they conspired, and killed
him. How he cried out from thirst there on that ugliest
cross.

Then I remember her story: One peacock in full color:
a kaleidoscope.

      That's Christ, all right, returning
to us: unexpectedly, with serendipity,
wonder, and brilliant struts. His never relenting
grace.

Sybil Pittman Estess

Where There's Smoke

(for Jack Bedell)

I leave the hospital the day before Thanksgiving.
I have been lying around, preparing for Advent.

Today is the twentieth day. Soon Christmas. Tomorrow
I see another M.D. This afternoon, outside, I paint

a wire rooster bright blue, my favorite shade.
He had been white. A pot of still-blooming white

begonias on his back in my garden. I try to light
my midget clay chimenea, but the fire is hard to stoke.

The opening allows for only tiny chips of wood.
For a long time, just smoke out the top. Then a thin

finger-size flame. I wonder: Is this like love? Friendship?
God? All smoke? Never hot light? Now it's dark.

The outdoor fireplace is full of fire, the day
blackening. Then the orange coals. But the time

it took! Like my body is taking to heal, like some
love-deals. Soon it fails. All the while I sit reading

your book. Hoping for a friend to write poems to as
you had. For healing such as yours. And a real pal.

Emily's House

One summer I sit on the side
of Dickinson's Amherst house—
not going in. Sunday. Locked.

But I wait in sun, looking up,
imagining her in light linen
gazing back at me. All is silent

except the loud distance between
her and me. How she has been there
speaks noisily—as I see a huge rat.

He runs on an upstairs wire from
inside to out. He is ugly and fat,
as if he has eaten the eros Emily

keeps within white. Gray rat is like
a feral cat. As that rodent runs
away, I too quickly flee.

Sybil Pittman Estess

from
Manuevers

Bogalousa: a Louisiana Milltown

This could be Haiti,
except for the pines
surrounding this mill-town.

All downtown streets save one
are steaming frames
for multiple prints:

parched blocks of rotting,
raw shacks nearing their end.
The town clock

cannot be re-wound.
Bodies of once-arrested Blacks
no longer blend

with the gray of boards,
and jolt us,
as if we'd witnessed rats

spilling out from gutters,
ravenous, plague-bearing.
And the mill on Main Street—

how many days has it hovered?
Its steeple-stack churn
churning a putrid smoke,

its gray tin, grandfathered in
without regulatory controls,
forming a stinking fortress

not at all resembling Chartres.
It's Bogalousa's monument to
industry, to paper, cheap wages,

and "progress."
Here in south Louisiana,
where dark skin

hides from white,
king of pulpwood in thickets,
Crown Zellerbach rules.

In My Alice Blue Gown

(Poplarville, Mississippi: April, 1959)

I see the blood
after our late-night April prom:
red puddles on white-marble steps.
I'm sixteen—

I'm the soprano who sings
myriad romantic solos
with the prom-night band.
They say he raped her—

a white woman. They can't
take a chance on random justice,
with daughters, wives,
secretaries to protect.

The elected deputy sheriff
lays the jail-key on his desk
beside the courthouse's open windows,
where the jail is on the top floor.

The deputy rushes with the mob
into the cell and yells for no one
to notice or tell. Nobody does
but one female witness

who later blows her brains out.
But I already know—oh yes:
the world isn't good. And white
isn't white and black merely black.

My world's all color, counted
by chance. I'm white. Mack Parker's
black and it's Mississippi, 1959.
In high school next year

I'll be a senior.
Someday I'll leave Poplarville.
The cloudy world is open
but oh so scary:

I sing "In My Alice Blue Gown,"
a thirties' tune. What time is this,
and what red space must I run from—to
flee far enough away from here?

Sybil Pittman Estess

Wishes and Needs

Sometimes, I'm born in Boston.
I come of age in decrepit mansions,
bricked and blue-veined. A Japanese

garden circles a sculptured pool.
Inspired by my mother, professor
of Eastern art, I attend Madame de Trop's

school for girls. At eighteen, trickles
of Latin and Greek and Renaissance painting
flow from my brain, down the refined sinus

track into my classic nose and out of my
seasoned mouth. By twenty-one, I choose
for proper reasons either to research allergies

or to conduct the Paris Pops. Svelte,
each day I romp with African animals, swim
with Amazon fish from Brazil, until

all non-need wishes are filled.

The Laundry Lover

"Laundry seems to have an almost religious
importance, for many women."
    —Kathleen Norris, *The Cloister Walk*

"Oh, let there be nothing on earth but laundry...."
    —Richard Wilbur, "Love Calls Us to the
        Things of this World"

I'll try to learn to conserve, to be green.

Yet I love, more than most labors,
clothes washing. My mother left me
this legacy. "It really bestows the
illusion," an intruding friend says,
"of actually getting things done."

I agree. Yet to expurgate all my under¬
wear, to cleanse by baptism after
baptism ritual, those towels time
after time. To purge stains: dishcloths,
dust rags. What is more rewarding?

I have scoured clothes while camping,
slung cotton cloth over lines from pine
to aspen, from oak to birch. I have
rinsed tons of loads, tossing various
materials into American dryers. I have

soaked dirties on a fashionably old
gravel street, San Acacio, in Santa Fe.
Deposited them amid dust on adobe hut
yard walls, or coyote fences, decrepit
sticks. I've looped hand-wash over tubs
in England, Belgium, Germany. Across
w/c showers in Paris. Put my purified

panties outside in Holy Land wind
by Galilee, in Greece, Crete, Mexico.
Now, what laundress could be as lucky

as I am today (even blessed by all
three St. Theresas?) I have never been
privileged to wash in eastern Sicily
in May and June until now. Siracusa.
By this Mediterranean sea, across

from the ancient city, Ortiga (800 BCE).
Beside countless sailboats, sails white as
coral beneath this bluest water, with hues
of translucent green. Beside bright pink
and purple petunias. I have cleaned every

throw rug in this seaside villa, each pillow,
all pillowcases—every cleaning cloth—not
to mention the cats' (Peaches' and Alejandro's)
mats, or our own Texas beach towels
and unpacked clothes. I could grow

older here or even die in this Sicilian
large, high-ceiling, tile-floor house
with heavy dark European antiques. Dear
St. Zita of Lucca, patron of cleanliness,
I could be canonized too—just to wash!

Companioned

He with whom she cares to share her
hunk of broken bread. He

sits down by her side. They sip white
wine or red. Each sees

the sore elbow, new bruise, old scar.
The sore pock-marks made

from working, or poison-ivy, bee-sting,
the blood-vein swollen.

The fat lost, or new inch gained. They
sleep, maybe. On occasion

they fret. Mated, they know harbor here
in their chairs. They don't

have to talk. He finds her more
burdened there. Nights, he says,

"Go lightly, dear, without the cause or
weight of our companioned* day."

*From: *vino cum pane*: "wine with bread."
  Current: *cum pane*: "with bread."

Sybil Pittman Estess

Shells

Candace Snyder needs to build a snail-like
hard shell around her. Armor to take
the place of the right, tight boundaries
psychologists say she just must build.

Candy would not rush to class
thirty minutes early to meet her
student who probably missed thirty
days. Snyder would let her friend pick

herself up at the airport. Candace would
not be so "co-dependent": suffering
her son's sixth-grade science fair, or
her husband's insomnia. If she were

encased, who could see her? Candace
would not write notes to keep touch
with relatives and old friends. She
would not buy valentines nor waste

calories on chocolate any man gave.
The geraniums could take care of them-
selves, and the damned cat. (Who'd care
if this feline whined over cat food

she chooses not to like?) Grass could heal
its own chinch-bugs. She would, at least,
be intact and growing. Let it cut its own
blades. Snails crawl out of hard shells

only at night, and to devour. So would
she! Candy could eat only her favorite foods:
fruits, brown-rice, vegetables. (As for sex,
cell-splitting would suit her just fine.) Oh,

how relieved Candy would be not to be
confused in another. How she would love
unbendable walls. Yet when Snyder's heel hits
them, often, near gardens,

they are fragile. Snail shells break so easily,
Candy thinks to herself, when they die.

Sybil Pittman Estess

"Say a Little Prayer"

(Words of George Herbert Walker Bush to
Houston press: Houston's Super Bowl, 2004)

"Say a little prayer for our
youngsters serving over in Iraq
and then enjoy yourselves and
Houston. Have a good time as
I plan to do Sunday."

On the East End, Antonio Gonzales
loves his three kids. But he has
panic attacks. He also fights
diabetes and hides his mother-in-
law behind blinds inside his

rented house. He is glad not to be
a "coyote" anymore, to have a job.
Betsy, Menthi Dang, a boat person
from Saigon to Singapore, has a
bad back from lifting her brother

too long. All other males in her clan
were shot dead in that far away war.
Menthi cuts my hair, is married
to George, Bac Huang, who just got
laid off from his job. They wooed

in a refugee camp. Sent to Austria,
Bac mailed letters and checks three years.
Finally, he flew to where Menthi was:
Houston. They send salaries to Vietnam
but less since she felt that lump: her breast.

Other sufferers at M.D. Anderson
include Iraqis, Pakistanis, Iranians

with their own stories galore. (Even
from Bangalore.) Yes, new martini
and wine bars are here. Money, MacMansions—

more than most cities build. Our real estate
rises: countless condos on corners. Yet
River Oaks builds no mere mansions now,
but palaces in their place. So please, try to forget Enron—
K. Lay. O.K.? Then

"Say a little prayer for our youngsters
serving over in Iraq [including our own
brought back in boxes by black night
from there to here]. Then enjoy yourselves
and Houston." Here George Herbert

lives on a street neighbors blocked-off
by buying it, near the Galleria shopping, when
he and big Barbara are not summering
in Maine. Have a good time as he planned
to, and did—that certain great football day.

Blue Grandchild, Blue Sweater, Blue Heart

At the P.O. I see an African-American woman hobbling with age. She's with a frail, little girl. The old woman reveals to the clerk she's just eight days out of open-heart surgery (a by-pass, five valves), and intends to mail money and a letter to her son at the penitentiary in Huntsville. She needs him to send something back to her, but he won't have cash, so she means to pay for it ahead of time. Is this possible? It's hard for her to hear through the bullet-proof glass.

The little girl is motionless in her blue dress. The grandmother, who likewise has on a Madonna blue sweater, negotiates things with the clerk, then heads to the table (where I lick stamps) to fill out forms. The little girl writes a letter in pencil, in long hand, on a tablet with lines like she has in school. It blooms into a whole page, and the process is slow.

She gets anguished when she makes a mistake and asks if I can provide an eraser. I can't. She begins to whimper as if she'll cry. The grandmother comforts her, though the old woman, with labored breathing, is leaning on the table.

I think of what's in Huntsville, and it isn't good. I see the mother has a letter ready, her own. It's to her son. *God*, I think: *I have one! One son.* I don't go where I planned: K-Mart and the hardware. I listen in the car to Desert Storm war news. I go home, my head still full of the P.O. and my son. I write to you about her blue grandchild, blue sweater, blue heart.

House of Rifles

It was before Hurricane Ike
years ago. I toured the house
on the bayou. "For Sale." So upscale

it had a gray kitchen with all dark
marble, a disposal, trash compactor.
The sink window looked out at a blue

swimming pool, trimmed in blue tile.
The bathrooms also were blue, navy.
Navy-blue tile on the tubs. The grout

on the blue was gold. The house was
owned by a psychiatrist and his wife.
They were splitting up. They had moved

on out. The realtor said she would
show me the doctor's "study."
Before that, I had seen horror at the door:

a brown, stuffed Grizzly
who stood, claws up, greeting
us without cage. There were other

animals the doctor had killed
on his hunts: a tiger, a cougar,
a jaguar, three deer, an elk and a fox.

In his study, I expected some books.
Perhaps a Freudian couch for his
suffering patients whom he must

have tried unconsciously to help. Yet
what I found were forty—I counted
them—rifles on racks on the walls.

Sybil Pittman Estess

"And these do not include his
antique collections in banks,"
the realtor told me. In the same

room was a clothes rack, with wheels,
holding his wife's twelve fur coats—most
of them mink.

Wings as Wide as a Tall Person is Tall

I sit by the blue pool on a blue,
cool, clear day, talking on a cell
phone to my old California aunt
in her eighties in Sacramento.

Just then three gray pelicans
fly over the white nine-story condo
toward the brown gulf, in triangular
formation. "Oh my! How lovely!"

I exclaim. Aunt Martha asks me,
"Where are you?" We continue to chat
about my cousins, sixteen, and their
families and kids in that far-away state.

Martha is the only matriarch left to keep
up with our eighteen families' news.
The only one of six siblings alive, she
is old and cannot hear well. Yet

she likes it when I call her from Texas
and especially when we can talk
about something beautiful.
Then it happens: What I thought

was a flamingo, but is not—a
Roseate Spoonbill—soars high
in the opposite direction, wings
wide as a tall person is tall.

Toward land, probably its nest.
It flew away from the water to lift
its startling bright hue not downward
to darkness that has come here

Sybil Pittman Estess

now to the bereft island, south
of Houston. But up, up toward
that gold sun, a magnificent pink
against the most perfect sky-blue.

Denver's Cherry Creek

is in the middle of this city. Water has
a bike-and-walking path beside it for twenty-

six miles. Marathons are run here.
But we are here to be near

a hospital, since someone close
to me is now ill. We must stay here

in the out-patient motel a long
time. The creek gives me comfort,

often rabbits hop these green
lawns and gardens. On Friday evening,

I stroll alone by the stream, Cherry
Creek, in near darkness. Traffic stops

and goes at the light. Horns honk.
But the water rushes over the stones.

I look up from my sorrows to see a
doe, crossing the creek quickly

to hide in willows, a barrier between her
and me. Her small but fast fawn follows

not at all far behind. Not at all
exposed for long.

Sybil Pittman Estess

from
Labyrinth

The Crisis Angel

O.K., she said, I will get you through this.
Dressed in rosy pink, she kept pulling me
through multiplied crises, one after
the next. Would mother live? Wouldn't
she? Was I going to get there in time?
Which plane? What would I find?
(I'd never been in an ICU.)

      "Look,"
the angel said, "It's going to get worse
but you'll make it." I liked her a lot,
her dainty hair, yellow as corn-silk.
Her dress, immaculate, the color
of first wild spring rose. Her will, tough.
She wouldn't take a pill. No Miltown.
Didn't even drink white wine. I'd never
cared for pink before. Thought it meant
not being able to face what's real. "See,"
she said, "what it means to be fully female?
You'll be able to bend on the spot. You
can be a displaced person at the drop
of a hat—yet not forget who you are.

"Remember the Jews in Babylon? Prisoners
who wouldn't confess? Read about Lot's
wife, frozen because she looked back.
Recall Odysseus stuck on the island, he too
wanting to go home. Think of Penelope.
Job. (He refused to curse God even for
his wife.) Picture Christ. Did you know
I was there that day fanning his fever? Back
then, my garb was white and sexless. Now,
I am Eve, Esther, Marys—Mother, Magdalene."

She stayed with me, since I couldn't shed her.

We went to K-Mart, close to the hospital
and cheap. I bought some temporary clothes
to wear as captive. My exile. Everything
pink: pajamas, slacks, sweater for cool,
crystalline April there. Underwear. I have
learned that pink is powerful. And I am
growing my own puffy pink wings, sweet
as cotton candy. I am becoming my dear
crisis angel. I live in the instant. My husband,
son, city, house, job, clothes, garden, poems—
my life—are far away back home. But now,

I sit at the head of the bed of sick and dying.
I bind the red wounds of my relatives, friends.
I pray five times a day to nourish strength.
I praise. I sculpt and mold whatever comes.

Sybil Pittman Estess

Outside the Door at ICU

We all line up at 10:00 a.m. in silence,
waiting as if going before the throne of God,
who presides over the highest court on earth.

We do not know what we will find behind
these doors except soap and hot water to scrub
our hands. Beyond double doors, tubes,

bottles and electric monitors are not sleeping.
(This is the post-modern age of life in crisis saved
or prolonged.) We eye each other. No one smiles

or speaks but me. ("And yours?" I say. "Seventy
days." "Progress?" "She still doesn't know me."
"You have who?" "My wife in a car-wreck."

"Children?" "Three kids at home." "Are you working?"
"Yes. I leave and come here at six; ten; two; six; ten.")
We clock the hours when they will not lock us out.

The young black girl with lupus dies. Her family
of fourteen in the waiting room leaves.
The young man's wife still does not know him.

The old man's wife, who's been here eight months
with heart failure, does. He feeds her. On Tuesday
Mother responds, begins to breathe without machines.

We stop searching for her living will at home.
On Thursday she's wheeled out to her
penthouse room. Yesterday, as I passed ICU,

a young woman emerged. She screamed all the way
to a car, leaning on the shoulder of her young, male
friend. "Would you like to sit her down here

to calm her?" I say. "I'm alright! I'm alright!" The halls
echo as she walks and wails and sobs. He holds her.
They leave out the same automatic door that connects

us to the elevated parking garage, where
all the nine-month pregnant women and I
walk or waddle in.

I Have No Story / I Have No Tale

In The Great Depression in Mississippi,
her grandparents who owned
a cotton gin went broke that year,
1927, the Mexican boll weevil came.
Her own father, son-in-law with five
kids already, an itinerant preacher,

followed suit in Grapes of Wrath style.
They all tied mattresses on Model-T
tops and caravanned to California
looking for work. On the way, they
camped out, ate from cans, slept two
weeks under stars in Texas, New Mexico,

Arizona. She was six when she first
picked in cotton and orange fields.
They first lived in big canvas tents
she chose not ever in her life to recall.
She didn't remember the cots, either,
the ones her two living sisters did,

on which they first slept. She did see
she was the one who kept the three
younger kids—especially when
that last baby came. Their mom worked
in a peach cannery. "It wasn't like that,"
she contradicted them. "That would have

made us like migrant workers. We weren't."
"Yes, yes we were for a while."
"No," she said, "No. I was never that.
That's not my memory. Mine is something
else." "What?" they asked. "What? How is it
different?" "I don't know," she answered.

"I don't remember that far back. But I claim
none of that." So mother did not own
her own story. She wouldn't put her name
on her pain. Some other, perhaps—but
she didn't say, didn't know which.
Her history, then, was not that of her sisters,

which is my inheritance that I heard from them.
As for her, she lived in the moment,
the present being the only place she believed
people should stay. "Why look back?" she argued.
"Even if it ever happened, it might
or might not be true. Who knows what took place,

what's real? I don't. They don't. You don't.
Don't you agree?"

Houston, Back Alone

(After Columbia's fall)

From Denton to see my paralyzed, mute
mother. On Saturday, there, like Icarus,

Columbia's seven soared overhead, then
floated down like feathers. I overheard

the news from the nursing home's
priest. Last year, I remembered that

my husband's brother, a NASA director,
signed five of this crew's orders

to go. That morning at 8:00 a.m.,
I had talked to my cousin in Plano. She had

seen the silver bird, high, knew nothing.
Afterward, I walked the nursing home's lake

path around brown water, looked for brown
geese, always there. They were gone. . . . But before

the knowledge of this new sorrow,
I breathed endless blue (clear as September 11

in Manhattan) Texas air. Saw a man
on a motorized, happy-colored parasail

wave down to me, smiling. Saw a blue heron
I must have startled from its nest. It rose,

became as wide as a human body is long. Then
ascended up, up into the neutral, unknowing sky.

Today, speeding south on I-45
toward home, in my car, I see on the right

side of the road two yellow roped-off pieces
of the ship. Now there are 2,800 miles of glowing

charred debris.

Sybil Pittman Estess

My Mother's Doors

After Mother's first strokes, she'd watch
for me at the front door or in the wooden
porch glider of the Denton home
for assisted living.

Then that major stroke.
Those heavy doors we pushed to get
to her: paralyzed, waiting.

We wheeled her past doors
to bright caged birds so many
nursing homes buy.

She managed
to move her eyes, only. Later,
lungs collapsing,
no food tubes
for two weeks, motionless
but groaning so painfully that all
nurses on the bright hall wept,
Mother passed through her
last door at nearly midnight.

I am tempted
to want my mother back
waiting at doors
of all her Mississippi homes,
welcoming me
even if she cannot ever
again be whole.

Galveston

It's a fogged-in night in late November,
her birthday. One of Jane's friends just died.

She sits on a pied third floor balcony
over a loud, southern sea. The fiery ocean,

this fierce fog could be in California
or Devon, if it were not just Texas, fifty miles

from Jane's home. Multi-colored boardwalk lights
shine through like a long Christmas tree,

foretelling the holidays. This motel is built
on tall steel stilts drilled down through sand.

Jane came here to rest from land, to count
the rest of her life and to plan.

To listen, hear what certain seas say.
They say fog. They say white-topped water

mountains made by wind, by whatever else
makes patterned tide. They say rhythm.

Lightning flashes far beyond her—out near
specters of jutting oil rigs. At dawn, white gulls

circle, squawk, feed by her room's open door
where Jane Clare sits in clear air in a rose-flannel

robe sipping coffee. By the time the sun sears
at seven, the stirring sea has sent her secrets

it keeps. It tells her all the knowledge
on earth, in its loud, wordless way.

Sybil Pittman Estess

Years Later

"But we don't live our lives so much
as come to them," the story says. "As
people and things collect mysteriously

around us." How Heath collected around
Cath, or she around him, like the nuance
of fog that she loved. He loved her voice

and her care for his words. Heathcliff
loved what Catherine saw as her soul.
Now they would both be so old. Does she

imagine him, ever? Does she remind herself
how she once told him she could not live
without him? Before her death, which now seems

brief, and immaculate. Is it true: we do
not live our lives so much as come to them—
like an accident that is not one? (Why

did her father save him?) Like the lives
of the stars, moon, and sun—that time,
those moors, two too passionate pasts.

Perhaps All His Life

had led up to this. Perhaps all his life
has prepared Heathcliff for how to face her

on the heath. Who is he? And what must
he face? He who has loved too much since

Liverpool, has not demanded enough.
Catherine, whom he has tried to peck open—

as this bird, this red-headed woodpecker,
tries to peck open the tree.

When his father would not respond,
he should have learned how to let go.

When his mother did not praise him, he should
have relinquished his obsession with accolades.

Is Heath forgoing it only now? He pats
his own back, lives without adoration.

The kinds of love and quantity he has craved.
See: he wills not to dream of Catherine. He wants

to rest, nights and days.

Sybil Pittman Estess

Likenesses

In the image Heathcliff holds,
she is a mirror. In his undying

vision, he kisses her toes, calves,
breasts in some hidden way.

He rubs her aching elbows.
He knows this: she would have grown

older, distant and gray. (Perhaps
someday she will be with him, but how?)

Even now, she speaks another
language: death. No, all things about

the two of them were always so remote.
They both knew. But Catherine's other

realm he can't see. Her stasis
mends desire. Before, craving nothing

at all, except his black grin. And what
sin he seemed to see or say. All that

quick newness they were and gave so
freely to their own likenesses. Yesterday.

Withering Script

Casually, Heathcliff has Catherine cornered by
candle-light, margaritas and whiskey. No other
souls in the barroom. She sits with her back

to West Gray Street. Windows show sunset.
This is October autumn. In fall, two
years past, all Act II began. They speak

of the three acts of them: beginning, middle
and end. "In the middle, you were in love
with me," Cath says. "Act I and Act II," Heath

answers, "are both done." No, she hadn't intended
to weep, to keep folding and unfolding her
paper napkin until she had torn it to bits.

"No," she says, "we are still in Act II."
True, there has been no curtain. Middles move
upward, then crescendo. Act IIIs all start

to slide straight down to denouement.
"And you?" Heath asks. "Your heart?"
"It could be," Cath answers, "I have loved you.

It could be I still do even now." Yet.... They are
losing youth. Their real lives have a hundred
twists: Edgar's moors, houses, their past

status quos, loves, locations. Two questions:
"If Act I is over, as agreed, will Act III simply
come as it can?" (Or will Act II never end?)

Sybil Pittman Estess

Rhymes on Albuquerque

What a clear, cool night in Albuquerque.
Old Town's not at all cold for February.

Since sixteen, working in Santa Fe, Cath has
loved this desert. She thinks it's a treasure-trove

of turquoise, adobe, chili with dry
air and moonlight. Tonight, winter sky

does not disappoint. But she's far from home
in Houston, and her husband. She has roamed

from her demented mother, moved to Texas
now. Deep lack makes her hate this feckless

midnight. Silence in the high plains is so lonely.
The snow on the Sandia range (for only

her) such a waste—and her eros. Soon
she walks back to La Quinta, forlorn.

Tomorrow to the shops—the Navajo
and Zuni bright blue stones. The patio

at the Church Street Cafe where coffee is
piñon, delicious. Hot tamales sheer bliss.

But tonight, Catherine sees Venus, her star.
She wants Heathcliff to say, "Yes, you are."

My Love Affair with Diane Sawyer

Who's to say it's only a one-way street?
Maybe she intuits the fact that I love her.

Why do I? I am not lesbian, though
no doubt I project quite a lot. (They say,

"She's my good shadow.")
See: she's up every morning and looking

more than great by the time my feet hit floors.
She is gorgeous. (I crave her haircut!)

My husband, of course, says she's sexy—
as we sit sipping caffeine, surveying

how the Clintons have goofed, or George W.,
Arabs, Israelis. Another thing about Diane:

she is completely equal to her man—
her co-anchor. They sit side by side. No

patronizing—no Jane Pauley baby-doll. No
Walters who has grown too old and also

has a crooked mouth. Ms. Sawyer is so
totally cool. Can't you tell—she knows

everything on every issue,
goes into the hardest, hot-spot places

all over the globe. Arafat's office,
when she is drenching wet and rain has poured.

(She never even gets sick—no sniffles!)
She doesn't get panicked, as I do, flying.

Sybil Pittman Estess

She stopped an Israeli army convoy
by the side of the Jerusalem road

in her British khakis—her hair blowing
but never a ratty mess. She forges

into prisons. She comforts. She confronts.
She is one wonder woman! I love looking

at her clothes—and thank God for color
T.V. This morning she had on an aqua shell

blouse and black tights, black rubber-sole flats.
I often gaze (as my spouse does) at her long,

lovely legs, today covered. I found out
the reason. This woman wizard can dance—

on ice, outside ABC studio
in NYC on an ice rink. (Diane did

not seem too cold, since she is oh so
adaptable.) She's not the slightest bit

racist. She was dancing with an African-American
dance group. Not missing a beat. Knew each

turn to take, black topper-coat matching her
pants. The whole U.S. sees her—maybe even

the world. I want my hairdresser to make
my locks look like Diane's. I am thinking

of bleaching my hair blonde like hers. (Oh yes:
she's thin.) Diane is not even divorced,

and as far as I can see she has no issues
with men. Jane Pauley left her husband. Long

before that, poor Jessica Savitch drowned. Other
female anchors seem to suck up, or come on

much too strong, talk wrong, don't have
that raspy voice Diane has, driving my husband

wild. He sees her, I know, for childish sex.
To me Sawyer has everything a female should have

in the 21st century: fame, money, looks, brains,
power, guts, animus, all. I don't know

her score on wholeness or integration.
But as for TV she's A-1 for me.

Jesus at the Pagoda

Marching toward me are sixty National
Guardsmen with multi-pitched catcalls
assailing. Golfers on greens knock balls.

(It's Sunday afternoon. The poetry reading
is finished. I intend a long, lonely walk in
a Houston park. But our city is packed.)

So a teen-age biker almost bumps me.
Six girl joggers go by, puffing like fillies.
I hear cars honk, leaving the zoo:

Fords, Chevrolets, Mercedes stack at the stuck
red light. Beside the path, one tattooed Asian
practices Tai Chi. An African-American female

athlete teaches her partner warm-ups, circling
her thin arms, neck. Then *"¡Vamanos! ¡Vamanos!"*
dins a Latino mother to two toddlers digging in dirt.

Rose gardens burst upon view with bright yellow
tea roses, orange Floribunda, red Chrysler
Imperial, Crimson Glory, Pascali. Next

to these are purple thrift, pink Gerber daisies,
carnations, verbenas, zinnias. I say I will
plant all this in my own garden—but I must

have said this before. I catch sight of an Asian
wedding on a lawn: white tiered cake under a gold
pagoda on green St. Augustine grass. The crowd

and couple are amber-skinned, round-faced
with slanting black eyes. Is this brown bride
in flowing white gown and veil Shinto or

Buddhist? I wonder. What is that familiar music?
Then I hear it: their soft, Taiwanese Baptist
voices sing, "Softly and Tenderly Jesus

Is Calling," and "I'll Fly Away," in English.
"When the trumpet of the Lord shall sound
and time shall be no more...." It is only

March. I imagine November, December to
come with some cold, brown, managable
order I want desperately in Texas this spring.

But today
I keep walking into color and chaos.
Tai Chi juxtaposed against Jesus at the gold

pagoda. Converted Chinese amid Latinos.
My musings go into those sculptures of
Giacometti's thin and bony men, across

the street in the sculpture garden, people
who keep moving always. Like them,
I go on by the one routine I know:

left foot, right foot. Left, right, left.

Sybil Pittman Estess

Clear Fall Day

(During memorials for 9/11/2001)

Afterward she thinks of the poet Williams,
who wrote, "So much depends...."
On a September day. On clear air.

All instruments, check-points, seemed safe.
Everything, even the air, was fair. Yet it
was seen only one way. No white birds,

like spirit, appeared as they did to a poet
transforming his mere vision to sight.
(New summer farm-red.) No accidental

rain made one transparent raindrop that day.
That fall no one stopped by a road
to write. *This poem is against certainty.*

For the sadness of singleness, no rites.

Katrina's Black Eye

When each possession had been swept
away by wind or water, and the chaos labeled
3, 4, or 5, death came. Or displacement.
What was left to salvage? No house, clothes,
photo to hold or help heal. Some survivors
waved white or red "Save Us" flags for several days.
Sometimes someone came to those rags or signs
by small boats. But refugees, rebuffed, had been struck
by the eye.

So many now have been hosts to some
lost child recalling when waters climbed higher.
Lush green gardens gone, and trees are salt-
watered at best. (The whole of horror is
not just tossed bombs.) So where can they flee
next from Pass Christian, Bay St. Louis, Waveland,
Gulfport, Biloxi, Ocean Springs, or New Orleans?
The lucky ones, left with breath.

From South Mississippi

(January, 2006)

Skies are gray today, tepid
January. Down the short hill
where I walk every winter here
the greenest rye grass usually grows.
Deer who are feasting see me if I appear
late evenings or early at sunrise. So
today I descend, expect the same pasture
and fish pond.

But the whole hamlet, it seems, has been recast.
This field is now full of dead, uprooted oaks
someone burned here as trash. Stumps smoke.
This year I find only ash and waste. Beyond, brown
buck may hide and stare from deep
in pines that the August storm left,
but I cannot see them. On my trek
past dry and rotting debris
of vines and brush piled high from Katrina,
one crimson cardinal against all the rest—then

that shock of pure black.

Labyrinth, Fourteen Ways

When you walk it with another,

                        you are seldom lonely.

When you walk it,

                        there are other people

on their own path.

                  When you walk it with another,

you pay attention

                    to your path—not to theirs.

When you walk with care,

                   the two of you never collide.

When you walk it,

                      you must look and listen.

When you walk it,

                    you are by yourself—but not.

When you walk it,

                      you get to a still-point.

When you get there,

                    you are not finished yet.

When you arrive,

                 and rest at the rose center,

you must exit as

                 Christ did: down the Mount

of Transfiguration.

                        To Jerusalem.

When you walk it,

          you have to trek and work your way out.

from

Blue, Candled in January Sun

Pretending You Were Joseph

(for Sue Collier Daniel, 1941-2005)

You could consider your seven fat losses.
You could ponder the long lean years left.

You could count the rest of your exiled life
not double-crossed but an Egyptian-style feast

to be ceremoniously eaten. Too soon past.
You could discover that in any parched season

siblings, nearly forgotten and foreign, might knock
for the food of forgiveness. You could ask:

"In a famine of mercy must everyone fast?"

"Blowing Sand May Exist"

(Highway sign near Clovis, New Mexico)

All she knew was that grit got in her eye.
Her husband, who was driving, thought it
had been written by a frustrated philosopher.

He came straight home and wrote an essay—
forty pages—on all its possible meanings.
She had been meditating as they whizzed by.

She didn't even see it. "If it may exist,"
he reasoned, "it also may not."
We were out on the desert, like life.

We were out where we all need reminders
and signs. And after reading them we think
of heeding. Warned, we wait for the wind.

Sybil Pittman Estess

One Thing it Was

Of course it was animus projection
or neurosis. It was her search for God.
Her Dionysian-lack. A yen to frequent
artists, a weakness for Italian males.

Perhaps just a failure to pray?
Call it *recherché au temps perdu*
(they were fifty). It was her Dickinsonian
quest for spiritual bliss, a fatal infatuation.

It was her old trick of giving-in-order-
to-receive. Both of their failed bondings
at homes. Unfaithfulness, and guilt, and sin.
Unliberated leanings on the wrong men.

Fascination with fire and butterflies.
But then, after all labeling, fashionable
name-calling, blaming, nit-picking second
guesses, some simple, quite out-moded facts

remain: *one thing it was was love.*

Esther Decides

She was only a woman, and no more
than his latest wife who was commanded
not to come before him without the grant

he gave away, like candy to children.
Although she was beautiful, she had an
inner life she had harrowed a long time.

Often she danced with her soul mates, or she
meditated. Sometimes she prayed. Sometimes
she went to see her shrink. She paid the bills

herself and knew her animus. (Haunted
by the ghost of her lost father, she thought
she slew it every year on his death day,

begged him not to bother her much more.)
But when her cousin called her to act
for her people, for Yahweh, and for herself,

she pondered it in her heart, as Mary did
one distant day. Then Esther took Spirit,
pumped her lungs with it, breathed seven breaths.

So she walked straight ahead, content to be
a Jew at risk, with good breasts. She wanted
no heaven. She faced him, female to male.

He looked. He decided. But both could live
with themselves a long time after what they said.
Esther alone had caused them to choose. (Now

she tells her dead dad all this as they talk.)

Sybil Pittman Estess

Students Reading Together on a Bed

One black. One white. They lie on her bright-white
bed right next to the teacher's room in the boarding

house where the owner has a rule that two persons
of the opposite sex may not close the door.

One is fat, one thin—they've been good friends,
she says, since high school. It must be a short

story: freshman English text. The teacher overhears
the soft words chanted aloud. Sounds like O'Connor:

"...and he badly needed redemption...."
Something like that. Then, "He knew he wouldn't

find it in church." They, of course, are not
in church. They are not in the living room,

either—or even just on her light bed. They float
in the kernel of hot eros—only she doesn't know it.

The girl thinks she is helping him learn. She thinks
it is only an innocent land. She doesn't sense

the many minefields of touching—if not his
clothed genitals or his skin. The listener thinks

this is what beds for two are always about:
hunting for someone's hidden half—the unearthed,

not easily scraped. Hoping treasures are there to
take. Being drawn like a miner to what

(for lack of better words) we call the finer minerals of
(if not his or her body) someone's blue heart.

Keyboards in Terza Rima

Early each morning she writes to him from
Georgia. From Vermont, he answers her by noon.
At cocktail time they want to exchange some

onions, olives, or cherries. But quite soon
their clocks tick to powder, pajamas, sheets.
She teaches sociology. He moon–

lights after his day in math. All she meets
on her graphs and charts, everything he finds
in his figures say their years and feats

are likely not to last. What binds
them may be such facts. They met by accident
at Narragansett Bay: a meeting of like minds

that is rare. Both bodies, too, seem hell-bent
on dancing through two evenings in Memphis,
then Mississippi. They'll have the luggage sent:

over a hundred combined falls with that kiss
from some other past not quite forgotten
yet. Days, they ask the keyboard what love is—

is it laughable at their age—this skin
with goose bumps? Then they wonder, "What will
our several children say?" "What kind of sin

can all this cause? Who will pay the bill
or where would they live? How to keep their
current careers? Just as crucial, will

he burn her toast, break her heart? Would she dare
to tell him how to clean the sink? How long
would they have if they began now?" (Her hair

Sybil Pittman Estess

is graying.) They have no answers—right or wrong.
It is like asking if the two would critique
each other's prose—or if death would bring song

or pose problems. At dawn each one will reek
of their state. They'll fetch slippers, wonder where
their glasses are. Then they'll brush bridges sleek

with Close-Up. While quiet, down here,
a machine longs to tell them what they seek:
silent, somewhere, someone can surely care.

Undemonstrative

I was living happily in Boston when he called:
"Will you fly on a crow's back back to Houston?"

"I don't love you—romantically," I replied.
(I am not pretty and do not speak well.)

"No matter," he argued. "That will come."
I returned, and we had a lovely courtship, then

wedding. When people ask me, "Do you love
him?" I am honest. I say, "No, but he is

the best of good husbands so I can't complain."
Forty years together and I never loved

my first husband either. My background, I suppose.
It's my background: undemonstrative.

I don't remember my mother kissing
or hugging my brother, my sister, or me.

She was sort of…Victorian. But my sister
and I were close anyway. Since I married

her husband, I moved into her old house,
wear her old clothes he never removed.

Last week was her birthday. I saw myself
buried with her, felt her in my bones. But I,

who don't know about feelings, am content.
It hardly matters at all.

Sybil Pittman Estess

Coffee in Cazenovia

She sips coffee in Cazenovia
from a gold-daisied, Syracuse China cup.

She asks herself, What makes the soul grip?
Does it stick by taste? This thickly brewed bean—

the hot, sweet caffeine steaming. Or by smell?
Sniffs of French wine, mint tea, brie, roses, oil?

Later, that lake gleams in mid-August light. Those boats
bask in late summer's ease. Are loves bound tight

by sound, she considers? His silence. The gift of one
voice from her childhood? Their own boy baby's cry

that long night? Does touch determine Spirit?
Yours, ours, theirs, its, God's, pain's. Everything in

sight kisses, then shifts, she knows,
then some so dearly missed—after death.

Native on Land

When we descend from the Grand Canyon
on the cold eastern side, Highway 64,
toward the Little Colorado Gorge,

we come upon the vast Northeastern
Arizona flats named "Painted Desert"—
huge and barren, unspeakable

multi-colored space. Near the corners
before the road runs out, we go east
out across the freezing, poor reservation.

We stop at the roadside market in
zero weather: December 26. Here
Indian mothers and children,

grandmothers, grandchildren sell jewelry
as always. They have waited for hours
camping in old cars with heaters, hoping

some winter tourists will buy. At four
o'clock, I hand an old woman a twenty
and she fumbles for a five. Bracelet

on my arm, we take the road to Flagstaff,
a warm house off Country Club Drive. Before
we reach Wupatki monument and volcanic

Sunset Crater, to the right of our car
in the clear, mauve desert pre-sunset, white
San Francisco peaks appear. On the shoulder,

two young Navajo men stride. Their legs,
miles high, climb the sky. Their long, thick hair
shines black. I see it blowing, strong as the wind.

Sybil Pittman Estess

Rothko Chapel in Black and White

So you sit here in the black seeing the ambiguity
of pretending anything is black and white, just
that: you see it, or do not. You like him or love her
or you don't—and she you. You either remember
her or you won't. You've been here for an hour
looking at the black on white, hearing all the silence.
You have seen it from fourteen ways, at least. All
the colors hung on these hued walls. What you need
is someone to tell you what it really means:
this black, white, nothing. How it's as easy as that.

Catechumen at the Blue Pool

Paddling toward Jane, at twilight, is an old
nun in her life jacket, bright blue. Jane is
quiet for the day at the Catholic retreat.

Here women believe things are possible,
especially the "impossible." They start
with exercise on summer evenings before

any dim night of the soul. The lady
says she is glad Jane has come for the day
to pray—although Jane is Protestant.

She assumes never again will there be
a convent as big as this one. For God,
she claims, is a spirit of change. Acres

here in the city are gardened, Eden-like.
Geraniums, hibiscus, fountains, grottos,
paths wind everywhere to statues

of the virgin. The nun says she thanks Christ
all the time for Vatican II, floating folks
such as Jane and her together. She works

with cancer patients, trusts that the Lord
never notices what denomination any
suffering woman is, or dying man.

She hastens to say that parents should not
wait for the church, but teach God themselves
to their own. She pants words between breaths,

while stroking. It is good, Jane muses, the nun
does not swim alone. At her age, a body-buoy—blue
as Mary's mantilla—brings

Sybil Pittman Estess

brilliant company. Near fifty, Jane tries
laps when her aged confidante leaves her
in indigo silence. Jane wills to believe.

Icon Room at the Villa de Matél

Worshipers focus, as few of us ever do,
on a hub from which to leave this place,

the icon room at the convent—Villa de Matél.
Each chair is full. Lighted candles fill space

with scent. Not the same strong incense burning
in the meditation room now during 4:30 vespers.

This is subtler. Still as statues, they stare
at those saints. "Something will emerge," the nun

had told Louise. She is that tiny sister who sits
with her back so straight. Louise looks at the image

of Mary, made in Russia. She's having trouble
with her son, who is eighteen, confused.

"Treat him as an icon of chaos," the sister had said.
"Notice your own." Jesus sits on Mary's

lap when he was near seven years old, the age both
church and Piaget claim we become

accountable. They are shrouded with auras of red,
and round halos, gold. Blue rings at their wrists.

Their arms wide, their palms open and up.
Louise stares as long as she can. Then she

leaves the people there, motionless, still—as if they
are insane on this trafficked, fast-speeding globe.

Sybil Pittman Estess

Pondering Iconography

(Church of St. Francis, Waco, Texas)

The only Anglo, she enters in tennis shoes.
Then, guitar music begins and the Holy Spirit

prepares to descend in Spanish. Murals
of fourteen stations of the cross haunt nave walls.

Frescoed on baldachino are a series of progressive
paintings: Franciscans with large gold crosses,

like albatross swords. They conquer savage
Apaches who try to wound kind missionaries

with arrowheads and blows. But then, Indians
bow low to might and myth of cross and these

Christians. Worshippers go slowly through ritual until
Eucharist. She eats it though she is Episcopalian.

Rosaries remember Mary. Only one icon amid
white, lighted candles is dark: the Virgin of San Juan.

Her black straight hair falls from her head to hips,
to feet. Her dress is light blue and white. The rest,

all the Christs in all stations—even the resurrected
one above the altar—are Anglo men the Hispanic

congregants wish for but never know: patient,
kind, less demanding. Their Jesus, sadly,

is like snow, pallor white.

The Cemetery on the Hill
Behind the College in Brenham

As she walks fast among the dead, their bones
under this secular ground, she sees new stones

are not like the old poured and pocked ones.
Her shoes also are not like theirs, weighing tons.

So they wouldn't walk, as she does, to exercise—
not far from her classes—a new enterprise

at lunchtime. Deities, too, are different
nowadays. Ancients lately have been rent

like the veil of the temple once: in two
directions—out, deep within. And the new

faith way is walking, keeping the body fit
by Reeboks. Body's cathedral of soul, but it

isn't like Solomon's, nor like Notre Dame.
It doesn't reach high or wide. No, far from

it. She goes in circles surrounding this graveyard,
staying in motion, keeping up, her bard

is body, not spirit. She is not like this stuck
angel in rock past people put here. (No, our muck

is not fiery but icy cold: old ozone layer
bleeding. Most families split. Bayer

aspirin making ulcers. Our hurting heads
in PC's, more e-mail than hearts can read

or sort.) Does meditation seem mysterious
waste? Do we know God? Would the numinous

taste hot or brief or condensed enough for us,
an incensed though frozen generation? Thus

said a past prophet: "What does the Lord
require of you, oh [wo]man? To do good,

love mercy, walk humbly with God."
Now no other savior. Yet her real feet feel sod.

Ash Wednesday and the
Houston Anglican Priest

He doesn't know what the lilies are named.
He has owned them for seventeen years,

tropical as the bananas here in Houston. Pinch
the green, slick lily-leaf off, put it in dirt, see

how it flourishes. A parishioner gave him
two bunches in 1977. "No trouble," she said.

"You can't kill them." They haven't succumbed
in all this time. He's had at least three hundred.

Denise Levertov, who came to read to his
church after she was converted, took two back

to Palo Alto one March to keep. "Do they bloom?"
she wondered. "No," he said. "A pity," the poet peeped.

So today—Ash Wednesday—he goes to water
one gangly bunch in his study, by windows, near

the view of high rises. They are dry, have grown
long, winter fronds, rising high toward the sky.

He should have trimmed them through cold.
Now, like kings' crowns, lily points creep

up toward the ceiling. Almost ugly. Yet
for this Lent, flowers are there! Tiny, white,

alpine. Delicate lily blooms prove him a liar. "So like
our lives," the priest thinks. We wait

and wait, even as Jacob tarried to marry sweet Rachel.
We almost cease imagining miracles.

Sybil Pittman Estess

Years loom. Suddenly, patience pays
in white bloom.

Blooms from Bogotá

Chameleons have nervous breakdowns here
in all this endless color: purple, pink, vermilion

on Fannin Street in Houston. Since she moved
here, Lara has loved fondling, consuming such

loveliness. Every season has its own
scent, color and shape, hue and variety.

But today, when her plane lands in Bogotá,
she sees plastic bubbles blistering earth.

Football-field-size hot-houses. Millions.
Her Fannin Street flowers multiply perfectly

grown with chemicals in Columbia. Sown near
airports for easy export. But Ana Gomez's

South American fingers, toes, have turned black
as any coal miner's lungs. Irene Gomalez

vomits for days when they spray right
in her face. Maria Lopez's child has only

half of its head. It's said: wells are poisoned.
Mirror-like streams are soiled as soil is,

chastity ripped. Women workers take
to their beds. So blooms must grow without

them picking soon—the roses, the mums,
the glads. Yet Lara's home city, Houston,

craves beauty and brilliance as ever, and buying.
Blind millions will still stop, be seized, and shop.

Sybil Pittman Estess

Blue Field

(for Carol Jane Antill, August 24, 1942--December 5, 2014)

The day they sat down in someone's spring field
of bluebonnets in Texas last April was a Friday

near a town named "Roundtop." That dear day
was mostly like any other late in that month

that year. Yet they were there, where mostly
they are not. They were aware they were there,

mindful of flawless blue blooming by them.
Consummate friends smiled, posed the two

of them in the color: all blue as far as you cared
to hope or could see. Nothing else like this

crowning click could be in Texas this spring, like this
dearth of daily task. Then when the friends ate

late lunch at the Roundtop Cafe there where butter
was good but the waiter too fat, they were back

to their fact. They both checked their watches
that would not stop as they wished. But before,

they split fish with no conflict. Fried fresh, better than
they had hoped it would taste. Better, fairer

by far, their hour, day, way, a blue field.

Prayer for Her Hands

(After Mother's stroke; Fall, 2002)

All their hands were beautiful, like Hopkins'
"dappled things." Before thirty-nine, when
cancer killed her, my mother's youngest

sister used to squeeze lemon juice on her hands.
She bleached out brown and kept her hands soft.
Both of her breasts fell, but she kept her hands.

I wonder if she still loved them. Even at sixty,
now, I do not suffer age spots, like my mother's,
whose hands lie stroke-stiff, immobile. I won't

rub them out, try to hide spots if they come.
Hands, separate from the womb I might
lose or my breasts. Mother's feeling, her

painter's work, she has lost. My mom's
hands and her sisters' were like mine: sturdy
hands that have worked, scrubbed often,

cooked, washed old pots and pans. Hands,
stay with us, even clenched, as mother's
paralyzed hands are. Brindled, broken,

to our long end.

Daughter, Can You Hear Me?

When I call my mother, usually it's about triglycerides,
church, sometimes scripture or prayer. Or her
neighbors, the flowers, freezes, cold air. But yesterday

she had been to her doctor and driven back by herself forty
miles. What we talked about was something urgent,
something she desperately wanted

to tell me, something she had not anyone else, not even her
husband, to tell. It was the sunset, she said, and the white
cloud she had seen—how huge it was,

and how strange. How she watched it for thirty-some miles.
Saw all the shapes it took, the pink glow it became.
How she had never seen anything like it,

and how she had thought of little else since. How
she had dreamed of it, how she thanked God. How
she had wanted me to see, exactly, that scene.

There Are No Tigers

"There are no tigers in the back yard. She is
lying," he said to her mother about her when
she was three. Her father, who had a hard time

with flowers, all things to be grown, including
kids. He had come up on a farm earlier.
How he hated grass, even—having to mow it.

But the green things he despised most were
wiles. Imagination fits in her even when
she was that tiny tot with lots of space,

endless energy to see those big beasts,
growling. She was proud, too, when he hit
her for fibbing or racing by his mowing

machine that never cut down her tiny
vow not to tell him more tales. Now
she's near sixty. Those stripe-filled faces

petition her to play. Like haunts, they follow
for fun. She watches well, does not tell him,
dead, all wild things he could let her see

or say.

Library Sestina

(Mississippi, 1950; age 8)

Her mother always let her take the bus
to heaven for a nickel. In town she waited
with innocent breath, wondering alone where
was the nearest stop to the paradise library.
She walked some six or seven blocks away—
then the ascent up the circular, stone steps.

The Hardy Boys connived up those sky-high steps.
And Nancy Drew solved crime where the dear bus
ferried her. The Bobbsey Twins played far away
from her house. Seven days she had slowly waited
to meet them Saturday. That ivy-bricked library
was not like her bookless home. It was there where

Miss Librarian said "Shhhhh!" too loudly. (Nowhere
but here, she mused, could that lady live, so skinny!) Steps
raised her to creaky hardwood, the library—
floors glazed. Then green bindings boarded a bus
going slowly home with her. (Each week she waited
a Genesis-creation for giant tires taking her away.)

Every time she had to return to a plain life—away
from magic to her family—and also to where
most mysteries stayed unfixed, she still waited
to go once again to repose—up those steps
where she could see Susan B. Anthony (by bus).
Bound orange, Esther was also in the library.

And it was in the same old library
that she wrote MGM, mailed her letter away
to Hollywood and went back home by bus.
"You have made a movie of Moses, but where
is Esther's?" she composed. She had risen on steps

of stone to reach that protest. As she waited

patiently for a reply never arriving, she waited
turning new pages in the huge, high old library
still there (being renovated now)—those steps
still rising. Today, when she flees, goes far away
from her own flawed house, that library is where
she yearns to reach by her mind. No, by her bus!

But she's strayed. Oh, she's weighted, a long way away
from her lighted library with its bind. She lives where
she can't mount those steps. She finds it won't come—that bus.

Sybil Pittman Estess

Ordinarily

(On wars: Kosovo)

No real bonds between us. As my friends
and I talk at a conference about God,

somebody slits this baby's throat. Somebody
else takes its shoes, another its picture.

Still a fourth denies it. Then somebody
hacks off the old lady's right foot, the one

who lies left of her gray husband, shot.
Hardly anyone sees them rotting in woods.

What was it someone missed? Imagination?
Soul, sympathy or religion? I remember

the root: *Re-ligio*: to re-connect. I recall
what they say of the Reich: 1943. I re-think:

how no one did anything then too. I link
that to Hannah Arendt saying of Eichmann

what stunned her: he was ordinary folk,
she said, following ordinary orders

on merely non-extraordinary days.

Most China Chips

Her mother was at her house for holidays.
Mother's home gone now, her mind, memory.
All bright photos will not summon, call
what mother shuts out or has had shut.

Mother gets sick, pneumonia, while daughter
tends her. Then out of the blue, daughter
is struck too. The husband has gone
to his old, moldy folks, shut in. The grown

son gets pissed off over some money mix-up.
Then she dreams of him—as a three-year-old
toddler who needs her nourishing him. (Who
feeds whom?) Questions of all fine china—

which she loves to eat from, look at, fondle,
especially on Christmas, each Epiphany. When
few things seen unlighted. Then new January:
plain same cycle to Lent. What use is Limoges,

yesterday, memories, flawless present, history?
Mostly we consume toast, tea, life from chipped,
everyday, too common cups. Containers from
which some sustain serendipity and sole hope.

View of Twin Towers from Bleecker St.

(In the Village—for Miriam and Ted Perry))

They tower to the south, out the window.
Two weeks we stay, amazed, on Bleecker.
NYU seems happy, close by below.

We come to culture that July. Fellow
Friends lend us four rooms. So, seekers,
We see stalagmites. South out our bedroom window:

Tall towers. Night lights. We're awestruck. Though
They're stable, they sway. Cowered, weaker,
NYU appears happy—to be close-by. Below.

We learn the Big Apple, we think. But we're still callow
As we trade high NYC for low house, Upstate. Peekers,
We peeked daily to the south. Out the window

Early, each day. Finally, to one tower's top. I bellow,
"I have to get down!" You snap rivers. Meeker
(like NYU), I am content on the ground. Close by.

We worry about fire. But by plane? Highest hell—oh
Who could choose it? Quick! Run! Down! Quicker!
They tower to the South in our minds. Out that window.
Like NYU, we are some who saw them. Close by. Below.

Memory

(for Kathryn Moody: Maw)

Petals. Two ebbed peonies
Wane from stems to the table:

Pink. White. Pushy prime past.
Their drying tinges are like

Us when we were together.
Smelly with yesterday's fresh

Newness, now deepening. What
Stays? Nothing. Not even this

Spring will last.

Every Sorrow Can Be Borne

For Laura Guidry, Lois Stark, Becky Millikin,
Joan Alexander, Carolyn Clemson*

she said, "if you put it into a tale." At last,
all of Africa was loss for Dinesen: by fire,

a business woe, a marriage-mate, her title,
then her health, her best bond crashed.

Lost lions. Airy continent. Finally, a race.
The worst pain was to face a waste of passion.

Wandering in us all a thousand sagas say, "Tell."
Someone's history: her husband, or son. Budding

young beginnings did not stay. How he is
for her today as Africa was for Karen. Cut off.

Absence is that steeped, deep sadness stories
keep. Ties, like scars, don't heal. Yet are not lost.

*All friends who lost sons in their twenties.

Search for Perfect Blue

(After "The Blue Jar," by Isaac Dinesen)

Each day Lady Helena sought
pure color she claimed she knew
before her world was caught
in less than primary hue.

Her desire was for perfect blue
she thought her lover had. He slips
to the hard edge of their globe. True
to him still, she feels his far, soft lips

touch, draws him to her like the grip
of the pulled tides and the moon.
He lodges there—complete. Could she rip
this container? She sees him. So soon

nothing clear lasts of her hopeful start.
Yet one blue jar still eats her red heart.

Festina Lente

(honoring Mary Eileen Dobson)

Sarah's God is like a mule working slow plow
Through dirt, while she holds tight to the old,
Cracked, oak handle. She has seen many mules till.
She's heard relatives' tales of their plowing cotton

Or corn. Sarah supposes the soil is her life—
Blemish and blight without water
Or fire or air. She and God inch along,
Stop to wipe sweat. They harrow field-ground

Left. *Festina lente*: to make haste
Slowly, with no motor or rush. Speedless,
She and the dumb, neutered animal keep
To their furrow. We can imagine them

Held, harnessed, and freed.

from
Seeing the Desert Green

Massage on Christmas Eve

The country club's masseur teaches night courses
in sensuous, not "sensual," he says, massage.
His French accent thick as Crème Brûlée, explains that
"Sensuous is not the same as sex, mesdames, messieurs;
something more: the body…healing by hands.
More potent than medicines, *n'est-ce pas?*"

In his last class, like Noah,
Monsieur masseur groups us in twos, male-female.
Stripped to bikinis and g-strings,
we stretch face down on towels.
With my back to him, I never know my partner's name.
Yet for two nights, we touch unlike timid new lovers do:
compulsively, in ten-minute effleurages,
petrissages, frictions, roving from ribs
to buttocks to knee-backs, from forearms to fingers, taking
turns with the touching.

Later that year, when Mother comes to spend Christmas,
this silent night before the fire,
I'll give her one early gift,
before bells begin in downtown churches at midnight.

At first as a matter of course,
she won't have it.
Says it's too cold to take off her clothes,
that she can't lie still for ten minutes,
that rubbing would hurt the crick in her neck.

Even so, she dares to disrobe
and stand before me nearly naked.
All clocks count slowly backward.
Under my spell,
Mother lets me examine her thin body,
its hunched back and scattered, brown fibrous moles.

I hold the cold coconut oil in my palm to warm it,
then begin massaging her waist, as he told us.
I rub her hips lightly, above the pelvis,
which he said not to miss.
Moving up, I arrive at the spot
she says is her tensions: her neck.
She talks, says I'm doing it wrong, wrong,
and asks me questions I don't try to answer.

I move slowly to her shoulders, her upper arms,
thin-skinned, flabby.
At the wrists, I feel protruding bones
that will be there long after her skin is gone.
I finger the soft, blue veins,
the brown age spots on her hands.
I massage each crooked finger,
each long fingernail, painted red.
I rub and rub the rough scalp
under her coarse brown and gray hair.

I descend to her torso,
thighs, backs of her knees,
tips of her long, cold, arthritic feet.
My hands touch all ten painted toes.

Finally, the last four minutes are silence.
She's face down: no place to go.
In cathedrals, midnight mass is
beginning. The priests are serving,
to parishioners in their power.
Eucharist has its healing effect:
eating the dead host to unwrap it
by that yeasty ritual.
After this, can we consume each other again? Or
have hands healed us of all the old blames?

Sybil Pittman Estess

Are we two Marys, anointing one of our bodies for death?
Hunched over these bones that bore me,
I keep vigil at midnight
under moons making the windows silver
against brass by flames that illumine
my hands.

River's North Fork

I did not like moving this far.
Here near the glacier where we are reminded
how anything on earth can freeze too early:
gardens, berries, roots, love.

In the summer, so far north,
the sun was constant, hot as Africa's.
By winter solstice this September cold
will be so deadly dark.

Under the moon last night we drifted into winter.
Snow crept. Morning is silent and still.

Spring Death

(for my Dad)

The father hurts more than
his life allows.
He dies protesting.
His vision, once perfect,

grows strange. His hospital breath
is pure oxygen,
faking the life-flame,
making it burn.

Revived, his eyes
see his grown daughter,
then don't see her.
The first day

he manages to say,
"This time I almost went."
The second he demands
she tell him if there is hope.

Told, in evening, nothing holds.
Unmanned, he wheezes,
"Get my pill...please. The squirrels
are out early this year.

It's Febru...." Not true.
It is already March.
There are no squirrels.
The third night

his last words were
to his wife:
"Who are you?"

Rachel Weeps

(Laura Estess, 1963-1983)

"A voice was heard.
Rachel weeping for her children...."
—Jeremiah

Why the magi cart gold
we can imagine: all births
are regal—that of Rachel's

children, and the Christ-child. Even
the man who murdered Laura. We
comprehend frankincense, for

fathers offer their offspring
to God. But why myrrh?
To bear the stench of what

each cradle rocks? Old Mother,
your cries in Ramah reach beyond
ears in sacked Judah. Your wails echo

for all innocence that madmen will slay
through the ages. They mock birth, even
on Epiphany Feast, the day she died.

Two From Laurel

He is a farm boy, good with numbers,
who wants to be an accountant. In Chicago
there is a school
that can teach him. She, from Laurel,
plays the French horn in her father's church
and draws sketches.

Her dad doesn't like sketches;
his dad knows no numbers.
Her dad says, "Go to church."
His dad says, "Where's Chicago?
If it's north of Laurel,
boy, you don't need school."

For that contest to art school
she draws many sketches—
better than any other girl's in Laurel.
Like the numbers
he knew, they can win her Chicago—
take her from church.

One Sunday before church
she burns the note from the art school.
(It had come from Chicago
saying "First prize for your sketches.")
Both daddys say "No." But he clings to numbers,
and schools himself—meets her in Laurel.

At their wedding in Laurel
they marry in her father's church.
She never understands the numbers
he loves; rarely speaks of art school.
She seldom mentions the sketches
she hides. Each mourns the loss of Chicago.

Neither one goes to Chicago;
they live in Laurel
while she dreams sketches,
keeps going to church.
One day he dies. She enters
art school, remembers how
he'd loved numbers.

The second school prizes her sketches,
but she is a lonely number (one, only) in Laurel.
She sees his face in each church all the way to Chicago.

Grandmother Poem

Thirty years after your stroke,
you arise in a dream
as a brown Amazon friend.
I go all the way out to your lonely hut—
a hard trip—to see how you've lasted.

Your long hair is unbound, a primitive queen's.
Your bare, bony feet touch southern soil.
I watch you draw well-water, fill old gourds.
I follow you in your sweltering world.
At fifty you are old as

Methuselah's wife.
Your life is sun-ups, sun-downs.
Between each light, toil.
You seldom speak. Breakfast is chickens,
killed at dawn.

In the corn crib you strike a rattler.
At the wood stove,
you sweat in August dog-days.
Promethean, you heat irons
for your ironing by fire.

I hear your scream
when you step in red-hot coals
under your scalding wash pots.
Although I run dusty miles toward help,
the bad burn never heals.

I hold the blue-ring churn steady while you doze.
"It's a sin to laugh," you always say.
Old puritan grandmother,
you tell me you want to leave me
your gold wedding band.

You were young, joking,
last night when we whispered
unfinished murmurings
all through the moon.
Ring on my hand,

I dance with you, limping, till dawn.

Sybil Pittman Estess

Histories

Here in this electric kitchen, myths died.
Baby, asleep in Vicks vapor and antibiotics,
what boxtop shall I peel off for you?

My dad rode miles on mules to school.
Ran home when he saw a white cloud.
Mamaw taught him to fear:

storms, wild women—whose breasts covered the moon
out the window covering the barn—
swimming (he might go naked), and basketball.

Mother's papa preached Pentecostal hell.
Hell and hominy grits with clabber
were all she knew night-time was.

Her life caravanned to California
for gold
fields holding work.

But no narratives are left, little one.
I rode in wagons
only when your great granddaddy took me.

I was three when he died. Daddy sold cars.
Listen, my only child,
even old stories can't report hearts.

Father. Mother. Son.
Chipping off, like icebergs,
now we drift.

Directions

(Kayla Broussard, 1969-1978)

You knock at my back door in April.
You're the skinny, curly-haired girl
who once lived here.
You want to see your old house,
the pool where you learned to swim.

You were only four then.
At nine, out of school,
you ride your new bike,
drop it, hop in, floor-flop.
You struggle over four rooms—

on one leg.
Cancer in your small bones.
Your folks believe in being found
in Christ. I've seen what it costs.
Doctors' bills come to my mailbox, lost.

When I first walked in this house
signs on the walls said,
"He is Resurrection,"
"Easter is Always."
You played our old church organ

that day, later pumped with one leg,
tried "Jesus Saves" on the piano—
looked about you, crawled out.
It's been three days since you said,
"Where is death, mama?

When I go there
will God help me walk?"

Disconnection in Santa Barbara

He's left other places.
Her place seems O.K. to leave.
He thinks of it as soil he can return to.
He thinks of being invited,
from time to time, to come back.
He thinks lovers like habitual return.

Brushfires occur as the dry season comes.
He worries, of course.
He hears that one wind blackened her canyon.
There are long rainy times.
Mudslides. Some foundations give way.
Now he knows how quick she is
to find a new house.

Stained Glass

This Baptist church is her history:
marriages, immersions, death.
So like her to hope and hold to memory.
She wore a white dress
when they buried her husband,
requested the choir to sing,
"He's the fairest of ten thousand to my soul."

In stained glass she designed
a bird with ivory wings,
blue water below.
Above Him, blue-stained air.
In between them,

the static, green rind of earth.
The sun's four gold rays reach down
to tell us in these dark pews
we are healed.

Her gift awakens old notions
of Holy Ghost in some form—a dove.
This window is like one "at St. Peter's," she says.
I think of how Peter was like her
and like all of us:
needing soul to join betraying body.
Untouched by this descending,
soft and white flight,
never whole.

Sybil Pittman Estess

The Geese

They have an autumn pattern, a southern place
in fall. They know circles everywhere.

They form triangles and seem sure their honks
are heard by each other. They trust tomorrow

will be the same steady air. We know a thousand
threats could counter them in their plan. Yet, envy

them. Geese launch the same October every year.

Agía Galíni

(Southern Crete: 1983)

Like vultures bending over bones,
old women in black hover and squat to pick dry greens
shriveled by July heat
and light so bright that we veil with umbrellas, sunglasses, shawls.

Pines and cypress once shadowed this island.
Now bent olive trees rattle in wind-gusts that won't stop.
At noon in Vorizia,
I watch an old man, cursing, wash parts of an olive press.
"Some people leave home to see what they can become,"
I imagine he says.
He does not.
But Kazantzakis left, and Theotokopolis—
unlike this mother who leads an ass bearing her baby, waterjugs,
dust.

I've crossed oceans for the town Agía Galíni (Holy Serenity)
to see one cat stalk trash pails behind a cafe
where John Denver sings songs (cut in L.A.) about Colorado.
Here bare-breasted British, Norwegian, German girls sun them-
selves
as if Apollo can't go as far north as their misty seas.

Then at Knossós,
we tramp on the continent's oldest road
while Anna from Oxford, tired of med school, cleans rooms,
then picks field tomatoes
when the restless settle after the season these waiters hate.
Like blonde, pregnant Helena from Copenhagen,
who owns our cheap pension,
Anna is hooked by her dark, Greek fisherman.

For twenty-one nights, I imagine

Sybil Pittman Estess

Aphrodite rising in starry air over these ancient waters. But even
Zeus, born in the cave on Mt. Díkti,
fled long ago with Europa
who had said *adio* to Phoenicia.

Like many of us,
deities seldom sit quietly at home.

"Return soon," the telegram at the one-room P.O. says. So those
contented friends back by the fires call and call
to ask what we find when we go so far
away from them—just as we would ask the old gods.
All they could say is what
we must know: "We can't answer, can't come back."

Mastodon Teeth

Orange coral, tan sea-cork, fishnets
hang in curves over the Formica bar
of his hermit hut, the man from Racine,
a curator who's lived for seven years
on this beach-cliff in south Texas.
He scavenges the coral from the Caribbean,
perhaps Cancun. He shows us petrified wood,
as we fight off troops of mosquitos,
the fields of Texas expanding beyond us,
the "Danger"-marked sea below....
Three pieces he holds off until the end—
two five-inch mastodon teeth, one mammoth's bone.

The teeth are encrusted with nipple-like cusps
that make them bumpy and ugly and odd.
They aren't at all like teeth of a toy elephant,
or glassed, dated relics in some museum.
No, real mastodon teeth simply lie
in my quaking hands—casual remains of a monster,
picked up on an inaccessible shoreline
near Brazoria. The man keeps them with
a foot-long piece of the old pachyderm's bone.

Dear old beachcomber, you loosed fear in me
on that hot and itchy night under an August moon.
Fangs gnawed in my kneading nightmares,
and I waked knowing this: of all there was
of these beasts, only their teeth remain.

Sybil Pittman Estess

Sunset on the Bayou

(for the Challenger Seven)

Now dusk is on Houston: flat and breastless.
Not on Seattle, red-hilled Greensboro,
nor Concord, Kona, old Jerusalem—
those subtle or volcano slopes they could have climbed.

It's the last of January, virginal
until last Tuesday. It's 5:30 p.m.,
six weeks past winter solstice.
Soft southern deadness, broomstrawed and brown.

Sun, setting we say, is red placenta, edging
the child's promised sky not yet night.
Walking one block from my house,
I'm by the concreted, graffiti-marked bayou, circling this city,

churning rain debris, turtles, trash, tires,
unfound trapped bones—a woman's who drove off
in last year's rainstorm catastrophe.
Stars, boats, babies, all that goes forth here
will travel again—down, down such dark canals.

The Country Idiot

Not many remember him anymore, my cousin
who had epileptic fits in the bottoms of holes
and other abysses he had to be in
by necessity—like the life he was in
with no means to control. No medicine
that they could pay for or wanted to know about
for their son named Leon in that land, at that time.
Now that he is little more than a vague memory,
I still see the country men taunt him
to climb down the fresh-dug well
late that night. He swallowed his tongue
and his mouth foamed
when the loud crowd turned its head. I remember
the giggles, the jests, and how he grinned afterward,
as if having come through some trial,
some accomplishment. And it was:
his mere living. Another extravagance
from my red rural past—like my grandmother's house
with no bathroom, no electricity;
like the king snake she found in her dresser drawer once.
And like Leon's two brothers, also dead: one in a carwreck,
drunk doing ninety; the other burned
in the gasoline house fire.
(He only wanted to clean the paintbrushes
near the heater.) Each grave has a picture put by their
mother, my aunt. I was seven
and fresh from town when I fled,
so late, from Leon in black water
to grandmother's kitchen for her to cover
my eyes from Leon whom I hated,
Leon, who never missed Sunday School
once in his thirty-one years. Full mid-moons,
now I fear him.

Sybil Pittman Estess

Hurricane Camille

Sixty miles inland, winds clock 200.
In the eye of it, stillness.
Before, after, we shut our ears all night.
My mother grips a Bible as trees fall,
breaking like sticks.

At 7:00 a.m., skies are El Greco green,
then bright blue as August dawns.
Our homes without light or water.
Everything hot.
But by the bay, the tidal wave rises fifty feet.

They find babies tied high to trees
by fathers who had hoped.

Christmas of Origins

For years I harassed my husband each Christmas:
a lioness clawing his back. Like shepherds,
I was afraid for another reason.
I was afraid we'd miss the joy of the season—
tree-trimming, shopping, baking, parties,
angelic music, Santa Claus, cards.

So this time he's tamed me.
He's placed the tree by our window early,
first day of Advent, lined up oratorios,
played Bach and Handel's Messiah for
fourteen days straight. I can't complain.

Instead, I tell him that back in my family
Mama, holiday soldier, tramped from store door
to store door for weeks,
marking off twenty-six relatives far away
to whom we must mail gifts.

Childlike, she displayed her gems one by one
to my sister and me after school,
calling off kinfolks' names,
wondering if they'd like this treasure or
if they already had one.

Then the pleasure of wrapping:
no red bow too small for her clockmaker hands.
Fifty gifts under the magic tree for a week
before she had to box them.

The rest were wonderfully ours.
Daddy, kid-hearted, would peek, shake them, peek
again, say could we have just one early.
She'd answer, "No." They'd go at it, back and

Sybil Pittman Estess

forth, about why or why not, their young
daughters watching with grins.

When Christmas Eve came, Mama'd surrender,
so then we'd have just one to open
early for four of us.
Daddy would never be satisfied, and
they'd go to bed like two friends

arguing over whether he could or couldn't
stand it till morning. Daybreak:
he was butler waiting with waffles,
strawberries for Christmas color, coffee for
her in her covers if she preferred.

Cameras clicked. I wanted, of course,
never to miss this annual happiness.
Since Daddy died, with one beat,
when they were each in their forties,
breaking a rhythm certain as metronomes set,

I keep thinking the way I learned it from
them: if one misses Christmas
there may not be next time
when their great joy would visit again.

The Beach: Mother and Child

(Destin, Florida)

When I am a child,
white sand shapes more than castles.
I make cathedrals.
The white sea-foam is the host
I take in with my eyes for a secret, sacred
communion.

Thirty years later,
you mock my old, imagined, holy cosmos.
Son, you are just nineteen months
when you chastise this salty eucharist.

Seared early by mortal vanity,
at the edge of sand and sea elements,
you shake your small fist, crying, "No! No!"
as God and the ocean kiss and sin
against your barefoot toes.

Sybil Pittman Estess

Seeing the Desert Green

(Taft, California)

The coarse, wooden forty-foot cross
has stood here on this hill since my childhood.
We cousins foot-raced up to it like crusaders,
called it "home."
Crucifixion haunted the invisible "snipes" we hunted here.
I reach it again, huffing.
Its rood still shadows the town just below.

There, in one wire-fenced yard,
Grandmother combed each inch of surface
for me to savor sweetness of sweet peas,
the dry smell of geraniums in July
(so unlike wet aromas in gardens "back East"
where I lived in lushness all year).
Mother's mother migrated West,
raised flowers from prayer-rich dirt without top soil.

Few knew money here.
Out of last night, I heard a young woman
who lives with the rough-neck on the dust street cry,
"Won't somebody save me?"
Neon signs just down the block
blinked the blue message my forebears clung to:
"Jesus Saves."

Not sleeping,
I climbed up the slopes to Taft's top,
asking why am I here,
hoping to see something new
on this same, old, black-pocked horizon.
Out there only wood oil-well pumps
stood, hunched over, like witches brewing.
Now the San Joaquin Valley's

Like That

filled with those green patches.
But up here just before dawn,
the heat already smothers low Mohave hills.
Tumbleweeds flee like antelopes down banks.

Grandma gives her advice,
"Watch out for rattlesnakes."
She watched for miracles daily,
And every other year
Mama, Daddy, my sister and I were the miraculous,
driving southwest 2,000 miles through barrenness.

At seven o'clock I'm back down
in Aunt Virginia's sparse, sprinkled trees
seeking an answer:
Have souls been saved by such drought and dust?
I think of Christ in his forty-day desert trial.
Lonely, like Him, at noon I'll stop
at four parched graves in the plot—
grandmother, grandfather, uncle and aunt.

Seeing the desert green across the road,
I will wonder why I came back
and if irrigation pipes or Jesus nourishes
and saves the new scents of this forced farming:
alfalfa, Greek almonds, kiwis, apricots, citrus in season.

South of here, behind "The Ridge,"
L.A. sprawls: "worldly sin,"
as Mamaw always said of San Francisco.
But I've come here as a pilgrim,
crawling on bloody hands, knees.
St. Anthony, I am past forty.
Foolish like you, my desert fathers, mothers,
I wait in this dryness to drink.

Sybil Pittman Estess

Epilogue

What the Citizens of Texas Need

I'm not so sure what the citizens
need is passion.
I've been down to Palacios, have you?

I've spent a night in the Luther Hotel.
It is dead, finished as the fishing town,
ballroom, railway. Has one cafe

to eat fried cod in, or liver. I went on
Valentine's one year, so I had lots
of passion for poor Palacios. I began

to think I could live there, loving
water, breathing salt, sea air, skating
on the walkways by the bay. I could

eat in the cafe, wouldn't cook. I could
live in the Luther Hotel like a hobo,
two 1950s rooms rented for

summer to write poems in all day.
I've also been to Rockport. I tried to
rent a boat there for my son. I found one

at a marina, gently Gentiled them down. I
have traveled to Corpus, too, seen those
beaches by palm trees on boardwalks

swaying like seductive dancers. I went
to Bryan, found some caring persons there
as well. (They knew a gal who gagged on passion,

nearly died.) Most of all, I had a best friend
who grew up in Navasota. She needed
nothing if not tenderness from her own

father who raped her for ten years. He wasn't
short of heat.... Perhaps it isn't passion we need
here in devastated Texas, or anywhere on earth.

What we starve for is compassion, suffering with,
to guide us through solstices, darkness,
through our fifties, beyond.... Yearning

for something we wish to keep that's
endless, worthy,
maybe true.

Sybil Pittman Estess

Acknowledgements

Grateful acknowledgement to the following publications, where many of these poems appeared:

Adobe, Borderlands, Brigid's Place, Cedar Rock, Concho River Review, Down a Brown River, Embers, Forum, i.e., Journal of Texas Women Writers, Langdon Review of the Arts, Like Thunder, Louisiana Literature, Mellon Poetry Anthology, Mississippi Writers, Mutabilis, Passages North, The New Republic, New Texas, Odd Angles of Heaven, The Paris Review, Pecan Grove Review, Rising, Shenandoah, Texas in Poetry: 3, The Texas Review, Texas Women Writers, Twenty-Four, Western Humanities Review, Whiskey Island, Windhover, Women's Journal

Thanks

I want to thank Pamela Booton for accepting the book for Alamo Bay Press, Lowell Mick White for his patient attention to my tedious editings and re-editings, Suzanne Holsomeback for helping me to edit, as well as Ted L. Estess. And I want to thank my poetry group of 13 years for helping me critique many of the poems in the book: Dom Zuccone, Sally Ridgway, Vivian Marcias, Laura Guidry, Kelly Patton, Varsha Shah, and all the others who have passed in and out of our excellent group.

About the Author

SYBIL PITTMAN ESTESS was born in Hattiesburg, Mississippi, and has degrees from Baylor University, the University of Kentucky, and Syracuse University. She is the author of four books of poetry: *Maneuvers, Labyrinth, Seeing the Desert Green*, and *Blue, Candled in January Sun*. She has also co-edited a collection of criticism on Elizabeth Bishop, *Elizabeth Bishop and Her Art*, and has co-written a multi-genre creative writing textbook, *In a Field of Words*. She has published well over 100 literary critical essays, reviews, poems, and editorials in journals, magazines, and newspapers including *Paris Review, The Texas Review, descant, Concho River Review, Louisiana Literature, Shenandoah, Borderlands, Southern Poetry Review, The Southern Review, Manhattan Review, The Mississippi Review, The Jewish Herald Voice*, and *The Houston Chronicle*.

Estess has lived in Houston with her spouse, Dr. Ted L. Estess, for thirty-seven years. She is the mother of one son, Benjamin Barrett, and the grandmother of two granddaughters, Himma Lynn Estess and Zollie Be Estess, both of whose mother is Briana Jean Bassler.

Praise
for the poetry of

Sybil Pittman Estess

"It is rare to encounter a poet as consistent as Sybil Pittman Estess. Poem after poem is achieved fully, to be appreciated by its audiences. This poetry book is to be savored and saved."
> —Robert Phillips, author of *Spinach Days*, retired Head of Creative Writing and John and Rebecca Moores Professor of English, University of Houston

"These poems offer a moving exploration of love and loss: close and personal, yet never sentimental. The poet's perceptions employ her intimate connection to nature and literature. Estess's insights or epiphanies resonate long after reading her poems."
> —Miriam Moody Perry, Award-winning English teacher, Middlebury, Vermont

"Ever since I read Sybil Estess's first book of poetry, *Seeing the Desert Green*, I have looked forward to reading her subsequent books. *Like That* is her fifth book of poetry and a worthy addition to the previous four."
> —Harrison Kohler, Attorney, Atlanta, Georgia.

CPSIA information can be obtained at www.ICGtesting.com
Printed in the USA
LVOW04s0601150415

434661LV00007B/27/P